By the same author

Women's Fiction

Eve White
Fey
For Love or Money
Heart's Desire
Love & Other Oddities
Quiddity (2013 Edition)
Spontaneous Combustion
Synergy

Dark Fiction

Away with the Fairies
The Darkness Inside
Distance
Into the Depths
The Liquid Room
Minos
Rise of the Bloodline
Sub-Zero

Other Fiction

Brian the Vampire (under Ed Page)
The Dream Factory (under Ed Page)
Greetings from the Edge of Nowhere (under Ed Page)
Lukewarm Bathwater or Apocalypse? (under Ed Page
My Life as an Alien
Orc: It's Not Easy Being Green (under Ed Page)
The Red Brick Road
Where Seagulls Fly (2013 Edition)

Poetry & Prose

The Light Within: Poetry of Oneness Book One
Open Your Wings: Poetry of Oneness Book Two

Non-Fiction

Everyday Magic
Gothic Fantasy: The Films of Tim Burton
Handbook for the Living Dead (under R.I.Peace)
Horribly Awkward: The New Funny Bone
Intuition: A User's Guide
Ordinary Heroes: The Films of Danny Boyle
Quintessential Tarantino
There is Only Now

Poetry of Love Book One: Twin Flames

Poetry of Love Book Two: Sacred Waters

Poetry of Love Book Three: Night Whispers

By Edwin Page

Five Wishes

Individual Poetry of Love books first published to Kindle in 2012
by Red Pill Publications, UK

First published to paperback as a combined book in 2014
by Five Wishes

This paperback is the amalgamation of the Poetry of Love books by Edwin Page that are available on Kindle. It therefore contains three parts that retain the names of the original releases.

Book One

Twin Flames

After winter must come spring,
Softly scented and robed in pale blossom,
Caressed by gentle rains
As butterflies take to the wing,
Birds singing in nesting delight
As the tight grip of the barren chill
Thaws beneath the growing heat of the sun,
And we dance through meadows of lush green,
Speckled with wild flowers
Kissing our feet with lips moistened by morning dew,
Our hearts singing the glory of life anew,
As we pause beside a stream
That gurgles like a babe in arms,
Calmly gathering our reflection
Into its sparkling embrace,
As we embrace each other upon the bank,
Thankful for the love now found,
Thankful for the spring now awakened
Within our hearts and lives.

A spell woven with a thread of words,

Pale strands like spider's silk,

Alive with sparks of blue energy,

Dancing and skipping along the fibres

That encapsulate my heart in warmth.

These words are yours and mine,

Entwining in a double helix embrace,

A new life created by our union,

A new breath taken with gratitude,

The words becoming a song of wonder,

The threads turning golden as they quiver

With the magic of our love.

I swim in the ocean of your soul,

Feel the warm waters of your being

Stroking my existence as they envelop me,

Holding me like a rippling blanket of silk,

Wrapping me in the wonder

Of your sustaining depths,

Where currents of creativity and desire

Entwine so seductively,

My arms opening to embrace

Your ocean of my contentment.

Like butterflies, we flit on the breeze,
Delicate wings lifted on invisible currents,
As we dance together in the sunshine,
In a harmony of fluttering delight,
The vibrant colours of who we are
Caressed by the sigh of each other's beating wings,
Dancing together and yet in liberty,
Through the spontaneity of each moment,
The dance an expression of who we are,
As we rise into the sky without restriction,
Finding our true potential,
Wings open wide as we inspire each other to dance on,
Exploring the garden of life in a union beyond boundaries.

Like butterflies, we flit on the breeze
And dance in the sunshine of our love.

You are the warmth and glory of summer,

You are the contemplation and fruitfulness of autumn,

You are the clarity and succulent darkness of winter,

You are the splendour and vivacity of spring.

You are all my seasons,

My Earth goddess, my love.

My thoughts circle her
Through every waking moment,
Flowing into her with sweet certainty,
She the well of my love,
The spring of my heart,
The merest smile upon her lips able to sustain me,
Though it calls to me across space and time
And my arms reach out to the emptiness before me,
Longing to touch her reality,
My heart aching with the yearning only true love can know,
Only we can know, my love, my life,
For we are united and yet distant,
Twin flames wishing to embrace
And never be parted again.

Her spirit swims in the calm waters of my soul,
The ripples of her presence
Spreading through me like a shiver of pleasure,
As she shimmers in the light
Which shines from my heart,
The waters purified by her,
The waters purifying her,
As the currents of tomorrow
Draw us together today.

The Light of My Heart

When you shed a tear of sadness,

I will kiss it from your cheek,

When you frown because of hardship,

I will give you my smile,

When the darkness pulls about you,

I will shine the light of my heart.

Twin flames, we will keep each other's light burning,

We will share each other's warmth,

Secure in our lover's union.

Filled With Your Song

My heart is graced by your presence,
As you dance through it's halls,
Gown of white trailing,
Its silken passing like a caress,
Making my heart tremble
As you sing,
The song echoing
Through every recess,
Not only of my heart,
But of my entire being,
For I am filled with your light
And our love.

Home

I call you home, my love, my life,

I call you to my lips, to the embrace of my heart,

Which sings a song,

The ballad of a love eternal,

A love that has burned since the dawn of creation,

Waiting to be revealed in time's unfolding,

To find its home in us, my love, my life.

To find its song lifting our wings,

The present our dominion of wonder,

Which will touch the future with the light

Of our twin flames.

I call you home, my love, my life,

For home is where I'll be

When you hold me in your arms.

I will caress your pain,

And in acceptance it will lose its power,

Become a memory

As we become the moment,

As we let go of fear,

Walk hand in hand,

Surrounded by the light

Of all that we share;

Our everything.

♥♥♥

The song of our love has echoed through all time,

Calling this universe into being,

Giving birth to all that is

So that our flames can unite,

Can burn so brightly

That even the darkest reaches of the heavens

Will be touched by our light.

She takes possession of all my yesterdays,

Cleanses the past with the wonder of now,

Her light vanquishing every lingering shadow,

As the songs of old flames

Fade and are replaced by our flame of union.

All that I am and all I will be is yours.

To you I give my life,

I give all of me,

I am yours.

I SEE You

I see my reflection in your eyes,
Hear my heartbeat in yours,
sense my soul within you.

We are one,
United in a dance of love,
Seeing each other's truth in the reality of Now.

You Are Everything and Everything is You

The shadow of a butterfly
Passed across my eyes,
And in its sighing beauty I recognised you, my love.

The touch of the sun
Lay softly upon my skin,
And in its warming caress I recognised you, my life.

The sound of the ocean
Drifted calmly across the beach,
And in its whispering rhythm I recognised you, my breath.

The unity of existence
Filled my heart with joy,
And in its loving Oneness I recognised you, my everything.

I see you and feel you everywhere, for you are the beauty in all things and in you this beauty is expressed so profoundly to my heart.

Your Kingdom

You coarse through my veins,
More vital than my life's blood,
You, my oxygen,
My very breath,
I inhale you and close my eyes in contentment,
Feeling you within,
I exhale you in my words and actions,
My inspired expression filled with your presence.

I place my hand to my chest and know
This is your kingdom;
This heart and body,
This mind and soul,
Are your home made glorious by your light.

You are my everything,
And my everything is yours, my love.

My heart is infused with the passion
Of a love divine,
Which words inadequately imprison
In inky lines,
This a love that knows no bounds,
And yet is caged in language,
Until the day we meet,
That day when destiny finds fulfilment,
When we find our connection complete,
In each other's arms.

I am naked before her,

Stripped of all the masks I wear,

My heart exposed in the clarity

Of a love that cannot be fought

Or denied, a love so powerful

That the world could gain deliverance

In its embrace, as I find

Deliverance in your embrace,

My sweet love.

If I could touch you now,
It would be such a touch
As could wash you clean.

If I could kiss you now,
It would be such a kiss
As could make you sigh forevermore.

If I could hold you now,
I would never let you go.

This love has changed everything. I rise with a new sense of purpose, a purpose which gravitates around you, my love, around us, my life. I find you existing within me like a love song, your presence within me singing through every instant. Your song is my song and it will last forever. We will sing it to the world, our voices in beautiful harmony. You have awoken me to this glorious tune and I feel the rhythm of your heartbeat in every beat of my own heart. I feel your every breath in my breath. I feel your love entwined with mine as we dance to the song of our union. As we ask for acceptance of all that we are and it is granted without condition.

My heart is a glittering cascade
Of love's divine spring,
Which you have reawakened within me,
Caused to pour forth with such vigour,
With such sparkling beauty,
The waters of this spring
Like a robe of shining glory
Worn by my heart,
Which beats true and strong,
Which pulses your name,
You, the song of my soul,
You, the source of the spring
That nourishes me now and for the rest of my days.

I give you the gift of me,

All that I am and all I will become,

I open my arms in abandonment,

Releasing myself to your will,

To our love,

Letting go of myself in order to find my true self,

That which is defined by us,

That which is entwined with you,

A man illuminated

By a love so profound,

A man transformed, rejuvenated,

By the gift that is you.

Sparks of white fire erupt from my heart,
My chest a cavity of blinding beauty,
Aglow for all to see,
As if I hold the sun within my breast,
Burning with the ferocity of a love so strong
That it consumes me,
Fills me,
My flesh and bone becoming transparent,
My veins turning golden beneath my skin,
As the fire spreads through my being,
My body aglow,
My head thrown back and arms outstretched,
As I become a being of pure light,
Radiant and shining pure,
Shining with the light of our love,
With the light that is you.

If we could share silence it would be filled with everything we want to say. If we could remain wordless we would learn each other's truth. If we could hold each other we would have discovered a language beyond any we could ever speak.

My heart pulses to the rhythm of your existence, the beat of our love, pumping its sustaining life through my trembling body, as I anticipate your touch, long for your caress, that reaches into me and touches my depths, enlivening the pulse which carries your name.

I kiss your warm flesh,

Place my lips upon every inch

Of your seductive body,

As you lie naked before me,

Watching every caress,

Every exploration of your physicality,

My fingertips tracing patterns

Across your yearning skin,

Your breathing heavy

With building pleasure,

As I savour each curve, each touch,

Your body alive with tingling ecstasy,

Back arcing, body lifting

In a request for more,

In need of my attentions,

As I lick along your inner thigh,

A trail of saliva left cooling upon your skin,

Tongue passing between your legs,

Pushing between your lips,

I taste your longing and my heart thunders,

(continued)

My thumb making sparks of electricity
Jolt through every inch
Of your screaming, needing, wanting body,
My eyes drinking in your nudity,
Their depths filled with love and lust,
My desire for you burning fiercely
As I move up your body,
Place my lips to yours,
Your hand taking hold of me
In the trembling succulence of the moment,
Guiding me into you
In gently gasping penetration,
Our eyes locked in intimate connection,
The rhythm of our physical union the outward expression
Of a love profound and everlasting,
As we climb to the peak of release,
Then fall into each other's arms,
Bask in the fading sensations
And the beauty of the light we share,
Twin flames entwined and burning brightly.

You take my hand,

We begin to glow, shining brightly

As we become a beam of light,

Passing across the world,

Dancing upon rippling waters,

Skipping through the atmosphere,

Bringing light where there was darkness,

Our dazzling union sparkling

In the eyes of all who witness its beauty,

Illuminating their hearts and minds,

As we illuminate each other's.

You are the ocean of my desire,

The current of my love,

I am sustained by your waters,

My thirst quenched by you,

My soul cleansed by you,

All that you are accepted

And embraced by all that I am,

Our waters mingling,

Our waters becoming one.

Sunlight streams into my room,
Lays its warming touch upon the carpet,
Marking the passage of time
With its movement,
The sound of the wind
Pushing against the window,
As the shadows of plants
Dance in the brightness upon the floor.

I stare at the shadows of the plants,
Listen to the buffeting wind
As the day passes,
Thinking of you
As the sun moves around my room.

I am the stillness,

I am the silence,

In which the light of love waits

Beyond time.

♥♥♥

Behind the Veil

The illusion of distance

Stretches itself between us,

But there is no partition

In our love,

Or in the underlying truth of existence,

We are one and the same,

The perception of separation

Merely a veil,

Which can be pulled back to find

Our twin flames

Burning as one.

White Light

Two flames dance in hypnotic beauty,
Winding about each other's warmth
In an embrace of light,
Flickering with increasing intensity
In the gentle breeze of whispered words,
Becoming one as the dance goes on,
Their light mingling in beauty,
In warmth and the realisation
That they were never truly separate,
That the two flames were always one,
Merely waiting
For the moment of truth's discovery,
For the moment of union
In the white heat of love.

When you have no breath
I will breathe for you.
When you have no strength
I will be your pillar.
When you have no smile
I will bring you joy.

I will be all I can be
For you, my love.
I will be your air and your sustenance,
I will be your heartbeat
And the sparkle in your eyes,
For all these things and more
You are to me.

State of Grace

I melt into you
In soft abandon,
Lost to the world
Within your arms,
Eyes closing
In grateful loss of self,
Content within the moment
That lasts forever,
Drifting in succulent silence,
Surrounded by your warmth.

We melt into each other
In moments of blissful peace,
Touching the divinity within us
Whose name is love.

Misted Union

We sit in the warmth of the bathwater,
Bubbles bursting softly in the hush,
Our skin glistening in the golden glow
Of candles scattered around the room,
Droplets of condensation calmly snaking
Down the misted window
Which obscures the fading light of the passing day,
Your head leant upon my shoulder
As my arms hold you,
Both lost in the succulent moments
Of our union.

I tenderly kiss your neck
And whisper 'I love you,'
Your heart gathering the words into its swollen embrace
As we melt into each other,
Cocooned in the warm glow of the misted room
And in the harmony of our shared breath.

Song of Love

My heart is filled with a love that has always been,
Its song beginning at the birth of time itself,
Whispering in the cold expanse of the universe
As stars came and went in the darkness,
Its harmony woven into the fabric of the world
As it coalesced into existence,
Waiting, waiting and always knowing
Its time would come.

Now its tune is sung by the beating of my heart,
And I know it has always been
Waiting, waiting and always knowing
We would discover its truth,
For our love was meant to be,
Our union is the song's harmony
And the harmony of two flames burning as one,
Shining brighter than any star in the vastness of all creation.

You are the poetry of my life,

The love song of my heart,

You are a vision of beauty

Beyond any masterpiece,

Your form more appealing

Than the most sensuous sculpture.

You are art and life,

You are breath and inspiration,

For you are the woman I love.

Within

The light within is always shifting,
A ball of energy infinite at its source,
Changing, moving, turning,
Dwelling within me and yet everywhere beyond,
Its beauty seen in all things,
Its light within every pair of eyes,
Within every quivering leaf and drop of dew,
Within the clouds and the stars glittering in the depths of space,
Yet no part ever truly separate,
All things as one within a single existence of energy,
And within that unity two intensities of the light coalesce,
Two sparks within the whole burning with increasing brightness
As they spin in increasing synchronisation,
As they mirror each other and draw closer through the fabric of time,
Each reflecting the other in the beauty of their dance,
Of their energy becoming interlocked,
Becoming a unity within unity,
A light within the light of all things,
A dance of twin flames finding recognition,

(*Within Continued*)

The purity of a shared vision,
Bringing their aspects of the one light together
In a connection of such rarity and wonder,
A profound love within the infinite love of the divine.

♥♥♥

The light in my eyes
Is the light of my love for you,
The song in my heart
Is sung in your name,
The warmth in my soul
Is the fire of our twin flames
Burning so brightly and with such beauty.

You are the light and the warmth,
You are the song and its reason,
You are the miracle
Of love.

Snowflake

A solitary snowflake
Tumbles from a sky of soft blue,
Caught in your glittering gaze
As it descends in the expectant hush,
Your soul sighing
As you follow its gentle approach,
Tears glistening in recognition
Of its complex simplicity,
The flake settling upon your lips
To melt in the warm caress.

I am the snowflake,
Within your embrace I melt away.

I hear your name in every heartbeat,

Long for you with every breath,

Other self of my reflection,

Vivid flame of all I desire,

Embracing me with your acceptance,

Your all embraced in equal measure,

Our love a bond of wondrous glory,

United we are one and blessed.

The mystery of life unfolds in gentle succulence,
As the cloak of my memories grows longer,
Its tail distant from my heels,
Becoming muddied as it stretches at my back,
Your face emblazoned upon my shoulders,
In fresh creation as your image flows from my heart and mind,
Your eyes rich with life and your smile alive,
Your beauty filled with vitality,
In comparison with the fading memories of the past
Which trail upon the flowing cloak,
Bleached of colour
When looking upon your existence in the truth of Now.

My love for you is a poem without end,

Comprised of only your name,

Your essence and beauty enfolded within this golden mantra,

Filling me with glorious light,

The source of which is the divine;

The spring of all true love,

Such as which we have found in the unfolding hands of destiny,

Its glory filling our hearts,

Now beating as one.

Take my hand and I will raise you up,
Will give you all I have to give,
To help you break from the chains of today,
To fly to the freedom of tomorrow,
With me by your side.

Take my hand and I will be yours,
For the rest of my days,
As we walk into a future filled with wonder,
The clouds at our backs,
The sun forever upon our faces.

Take my hand and I will take yours,
Together we will walk side by side,
In the light of love.

I gave you my heart
And with you it remains,
Until my remains are laid to rest.

I entwined my essence with yours
And our flames shall be forever united,
Even after the flames in my eyes have gone out.

All that I am is yours
And though I shall pass beyond this world,
In the eternity of the divine we will always be together.

❤❤❤

She is a healer,
Each word a balm soothing my very soul.
She is an inspiration,
Her every exhalation breathing life into me.
She is the woman I love,
Everything I am belongs to her.

I offer my wings
So you may fly,
So I may watch you vanish from sight,
Pass through the clouds
Into the realm of sunlight beyond,
Your wings touched with gold
As you soar and glide.

I offer my heart
So you may carry me with you,
And even though I remain upon the ground,
I will always know
A part of me is in your keeping.

I offer my love
So you may never feel alone
In endless skies of blue.

My love has no limit,

For its source is the infinite divine,

Which resides within and without,

This love for her its expression and glorious in its boundlessness,

As I offer all I am,

As I give all I can without condition or demand,

But simply to uplift and nourish,

To sustain and inspire,

She who is deserving of this and so much more,

She of such beauty I am left breathless and filled with longing,

She, the woman of my affection until my life is spent,

She, the light held in the fathoms of my oceanic eyes,

She, my other self.

The wondrous pool within
Shimmers and stirs, softly,
So softly, sunlight skipping
Upon its gentle ripples,
Eclipsed by the brightness
Held within its depths, the light
Of infinity, of love
That knows no bounds,
Running through us in streams
Originating from this divine pool, filling us
With the glory of God,
A glory that shines
In our hearts, our minds and our eyes.

My love for you is an aspect
Of this glory, this source
Which unites us all, its delta
Running through all things,
Linking us beyond space and time,
Where I hold you in adoration;

(continued)

Two drops of the whole
Merging within the pool,
Transfigured by a love deep and true,
In which we embrace for eternity,
Washed clean, shining beings
Entwined in the glory, in the light
In our love.

You taught my heart to sing again,

Like a young bird opening its wings

For the first flight of spring,

Rising on warm currents of love,

Its song resounding through the orchard of my life,

Which blossoms with your presence,

The air filled with fragrance,

As this heart of mine sings again

And flutters your name.

A song sung through the mists of time
Has found itself renewed,
As two spirits are rekindled
By destiny's guiding hands,
To entwine once again
In a love never lost or forgotten.

We are the ancient mysticism,
We are the newfound glory,
We are the intensity of the past
And the future's potential,
We are a beautiful union
Of all that we are.

Utopian Twilight

We sit together
And look out over the calm waters of the lake,
A contented silence hung about our shoulders
As we hold each other close,
Time lining our faces with its passing
But unable to dim the light in our eyes,
Our union a harmony of two spirits
Become one in the glory of love,
Our entwined existence radiant,
Illuminating the world
With its wonder,
As we sit in the tranquillity of life's twilight
And the sun gently sinks from the world,
Its last golden rays
Gently caressing our aged faces,
Briefly captured within the sparkle of our eyes,
Our smiles speaking of lives fulfilled.

Book Two

SACRED WATERS

I am exposed,

Open and bleeding words that speak of the essence of me,

Of what lies within.

I bare myself,

Lie naked before her in totality,

Giving all I have in the hope it is enough.

My heart and mind are entwined,

In this love that has the power to leave me helpless,

Everything I am lying prone on the sacrificial alter,

Of her eyes.

Her gravity pulls me in,
Is inescapable.

I tumble into her, helpless,
Vanishing beyond the event horizon of her eyes,

There is no escape attempted nor wished,
My only desire being to fall forever.

She is the beauty of every petal
That trembles breathlessly beneath the warming sun,
She is the wonder of the blue sky,
Striking in its clarity,
She is the sound of the ocean
As it caresses the shore in continual seduction,
She is the whole of creation,
Captured within her gaze and given life anew.

I am also a captive within her eyes,
As she breathes her warmth into me,
Swells my heart with her glory,
For she is the woman I love.

Everything

Her words are like starlight falling into my eyes,
Filling them with her distant light,
Captivating me with beauty that shines so bright,
Reflected in the depth of my dilated pupils,
Where her face resides through every waking hour,
Her essence within me and mine within her,
Two people becoming enfolded into each other
In the sublime wonder of love's true union.

❤❤❤

She is the dance of butterflies on the wing,
The swaying of golden corn beneath the summer sun,
She is the dewdrop glittering in the morning hush,
The rainbow of rain's passing,
She is all that is beauty,
She is all that is wonder,
She is all that I love,
The world within her eyes.

We lie together upon the hill in the silence of our contentment. The starlight sings as it falls into our eyes and the ocean wraps us in its gentle breathing. We are one in the darkness, the flush of making love still upon our faces as we savour every moment. We are cleansed of all our yesterdays. Newly born, we are children of our love.

The breeze strokes our hair and tingles the skin of our naked bodies. We cuddle close and feel each other's soft warmth. Turning to each other, we find the starlight captured within our eyes. With tenderness we kiss, our lips quivering like petals opening beneath the touch of the spring sun.

With a gentle sigh we fall into the depths of our universe eyes, surrendering all that we are to the love we share.

I drift in the universe of your gaze,

Lost in your limitless depth,

Wishing to forever remain

In the glittering heavens of your love,

The cosmos of your heart and soul,

Filled with lights of beauty

Shining within the firmament of your eyes.

There's more poetry in your eyes
Than I could ever hope to express in words,
There's more beauty in your smile
Than I could ever hope to capture upon canvas.
When I look within you I am blinded,
My inspiration a dull reflection of your light,
For it is the light of love
And has no need of words to find its expression,
No need of paints to show its beauty,
It is the divine within you
And you shine with its glory.

❤❤❤

I wrap my love around you,
In acceptance of all that you are,
And one day my arms will embrace you,
I will look into your eyes,
And simply say 'yes.'

She, My Liberty

Finding a heartbeat beside me,
In moments of waking calm
And the stillness of our room.

Walls fading away, retreating,
Star-spun sky revealed above
As I feel a new freedom of emotion and expression,
All barriers dissolving
As we lie in each other's arms.

I am liberated by her presence,
By her soft breath upon my skin,
Our warm bodies drawn close,
Vanquishing the chill which had settled within,
As we lay in our bed of contented silence,
Our sea of tranquillity,
Studded with the stars shining in our eyes.

My Sunshine

The sunshine kisses my lips with warm tenderness,
Its golden glow sparkling in my pupils,
Its touch filling me with joy,
Overwhelming me with the beauty of existence,
Tears of happiness welling in my eyes.

You are my sunshine, my love,
You are the warmth and the light,
You are the joy and the beauty,
The world gathered in your aspect,
It's wonder shining in your eyes.

I Hear Your Voice

You called my name in the darkness,
And I answered with the light of love,
That was reflected in your eyes.

I held you close in the chill,
As we huddled into the warmth
Of each other's presence.

Our pulsing hearts became entwined,
The darkness replaced by brightness,
The cold replaced by heat,
The world touched by the beauty
That we found within each other,
That we awakened in the wonder of our union.

Inescapable

My existence revolves around you, my love,
You; my gravity, my attraction,
My heart and mind drawn to you
With irresistible certainty,
As I release myself to this union,
Let myself fall
Into the glittering wonder of your eyes.

I can communicate with you without words,

Hold you without arms,

Caress you without lips,

All you need to do is look into my eyes,

There you will find me

Naked before you

To the depth of my soul,

Where the light of love shines brightly.

♥♥♥

Your enchanting eyes hold me captivated, bound in a spell of love, wrapped in eternity's embrace, foretold in the whispers of destiny, echoing through the corridors of time, where we have at last met, found each to be the other's reflection, seeing our true selves in each other's eyes, these watery depths holding the magic, of all that we are, as we see one another, in the light of the love we share, this enchantment that has always been and shall forever remain, for true love never dies.

There is never a moment

When you are not with me,

In my thoughts and within the comfort of my heart,

Its soft warmth gathered about you,

Healing your past as you heal mine,

Promising never to cage you,

But to give you the release of freedom,

Encouragement to open your wings,

So we may fly together,

Two hearts as one,

United in the light of our eyes

And the beauty that arises from our union,

The warm air of love and inspiration

Lifting us into the blue eternity,

Where we will dwell forevermore.

A New Dawn

The first light of dawn
Lays its pale fingers upon your nakedness,
As you lay sleeping beside me
And I take in the beauty of your restful form.

I reach out to gently touch you
With trembling fingertips,
Hardly daring to believe you are real,
That you are truly lying beside me.

I stroke your curves
In the softness of the waking day,
You stir in smiling pleasure,
Turning and opening your eyes.

We stare into each other's souls
As I continue to caress your warmth,
Your face aglow with contentment,
The new day filled with the whispers of love.

We lift into the endless blue
Of a cloudless sky,
Our wings shimmering
In the first rays of the sun,
That shine from the distant horizon
Where the sea and sky embrace.

Our wings stretch wide,
We glide on warm updrafts,
Silent as we hold each other's hands,
As we look into each other's eyes and nod,
Rising beyond the azure sky
To soar into the universe of potential.

There's nowhere I'd rather be

Than lost in your arms and your eyes,

Lost in the silence of understanding

That we share,

Lost on the ocean of our love,

For in being lost in you

I find myself.

My words are feeble

Compared with the poetry of your eyes,

The song of your smile.

My linguistic structures are but empty halls

Beside the fullness of your heart,

Which I hear beating across the ocean.

You are inspiration and creativity,

You are mother earth

And the ocean of my birth and death,

You are the truth of my existence.

My love, my life,

All I am is yours,

Though I may be but a shadow

Cast by your light.

In the Snow

She dances in the falling snow,
Pale flakes tumbling from soft blue clouds.

She turns and spins with arms wide,
Smile bright, laughter escaping her lips
With the mist of her warm breath,
Her shoes softly hidden
In the white blanket of the hush.

She dances in the soft flurries,
Flakes caressing her hair
And cascading down her shoulders,
Scarf fluttering with her movements,
As she looks at me, eyes alight
With happiness and love.

I am overwhelmed by the sight
Of the woman I love dancing in the snow,
Her feet moved by joy
And her laughter telling of its truth,
My heart melting like the flakes upon her pale cheeks.

The snow falls in the hush. There is the faintest whisper as each flake caresses the earth with crystal lips. The land fades to white in the darkness as two figures watch from the brow of the hill.

Their eyes glitter with the lights that shimmer across the wide bay and with an inner light filled with warmth, the chill of the night held at bay by the company they keep.

They watch the flakes fall, listen to their whispering. Silent figures. Content and still as the snow settles upon them, covers them in its blanket of purity, reflecting the glory within their hearts.

Nothing else exists. They are the infinity of each other's desire. They are the silence of contentment. They are the glory of companionship now lost forever from the world beneath a blanket of love.

They stand in the Japanese winter garden,
Arms about each other in a close embrace,
Snowflakes drifting in whispers from the dark sky,
The ground a serene blanket of purity.

They stare into each other's eyes in the sculptural night,
They lean in and kiss with tenderness,
Flakes in their hair glittering
In the light spilling from nearby buildings,
The gentle illumination eclipsed
By the brightness within their eyes;
A love eternal which fills the awed hush.

The snowflakes whisper two names as they fall;
Our names, my love, our names.

Jubilant fire arcs through his soul,
Sending sparks from his glittering eyes;
Energy, such energy as love can bring,
His heart a vessel filled with its glory,
Filled with her in swelling abandon,
Calling her name and touched by her grace,
He is consumed by her, his love,
Feeling the fire within, white with heat,
Bright with the warmth of a thousand suns
Which are contained within her eyes.

Sacred heart of my desire,

Blessed love of my every wish,

You alight upon my every breath,

I exhale you with every word,

All my thoughts made succulent

By these feelings so astounding,

So overwhelming, the wonder of your beauty

Filling me, inspiring every wordy flight,

My love, you give me wings

Of such majesty, raising me on high,

Stars glittering on my wings

As I soar into your eyes.

Your Embrace

The serenity of your arms calls to me,
Your eyes singing a loving serenade
As your embrace calms my soul,
Cleanses my past in the intoxication of your beauty,
Which shines from every aspect of your existence,
Blinding me to the world
As you become my universe,
Your arms my home,
A place of warm tenderness
Reflecting the heat of the love we share.

Dissolving

His kisses drift across her skin,

Lips cast in moonlight

Spilling from her eyes,

As she holds him captive in her gaze,

Trembling beneath his touch,

Body pleading to him,

Rising to meet his sensual caresses,

Their immediacy an intoxication,

Each touch the centre of her existence

As she melts into his presence and he into hers,

This a lover's union never to be undone.

Divine Embrace

She touched his soul with a finger of starlight
Reaching from the depths of her eyes.
She caressed his spirit with a sense of delight
Skipping on the curve of her smile.
She breathed on his skin with a fierce passion
Powered by the beat of her heart.
She kissed his lips with a lust pulsating
From the white heat between her legs.

Her touch, her caress,
Her kiss, her breath.

He was no more a man, but a god
In the intoxicating embrace of her love.

No words can say what my eyes long to tell you,
No sentence can hold the truth waiting within my arms,
Silence is all that we need
As we look into each other's eyes,
As we fall into each other's arms
And find that we are home.

The surf froths upon the beach as we walk in the rain,
The wind tugging at our wet hair,
Raindrops caressing our cheeks as we smile,
Hands held tight
In the silent communion of our souls,
Soaked clothes clinging to the nakedness beneath,
A nakedness we share upon our return to the house,
Stripping each other in the silence of longing,
Scattering kisses upon our damp skin
As the layers are peeled away,
To then embrace and find the warmth
Of each other's closeness,
Of each other's solidity for which we yearned for so long,
Gently lying together upon the bed,
Becoming lost in love's physical expression,
Our bodies writhing in the soft luxury
Of our flesh joined,
In the ultimate act of intimate contact,
Our desire finding release,
In moments consumed by the immediacy

(continued)

Of our closeness,

To eventually lie together

In the comfort of pleasure's passing,

Lost to the moment,

And the depths of each other's eyes.

♥♥♥

Into Your Eyes

I fall into the liquid domain of your eyes,

Bathe in the depth of their infinite oceans,

Adrift on their soft currents

And buoyed by the breeze of your smile,

Caressed by the warmth of your spirit,

The light of your love sparkling

Upon the gentle waves

Of all that you are.

Upon the Hill

You shake moonlight from your hair
As you stand naked on the hilltop,
The darkened world like a blanket at your feet,
The black velvet of the sky spun with stars,
Glittering in your eyes
As you look out over the wide bay,
Awash with the sounds of the ocean.

The soft pad of my steps
Is carried to you on the breeze,
You smile without turning as I approach,
My nakedness reflecting your own,
My arms encircling your waist
As my lips gently caress your neck,
The hush becoming a sigh of contentment.

I see you, yet I am distant,

I feel you, yet we are apart,

I place my hand to my chest

And feel your heartbeat,

I look into my eyes

And find you looking back at me,

You are by my side when I lay my head to rest,

You walk beside me through every day,

There is not a single breath

That does not contain you,

All I am is yours,

For this is love,

Without condition.

I see beyond the surface ripples

In the reflections of your eyes,

As we speak telepathically

In moments of profound connection,

No words able to express

The depths we fathom.

♥♥♥

The language of love slips from my eyes,

As they talk without need of words,

Communicate from the depths of my being,

Expressing more than I could ever hope to articulate,

As I gaze at you, my lover,

And the song within sings in the sparkle of my delight.

I want to caress you

With my fingers and my lips,

They'll speak to you in gentle touches,

Whispering my feelings in the hush,

Letting you hear the language of my desire,

Telling you of your beauty

As your eyes tell me of mine.

My heart is a supernova
In your nuclear presence,
Passionate fire dancing in our eyes,
My soul ripped from my body
By its desire to entwine with yours,
Words and images tumbling from my mind
In a torrent of inspiration.

All of me is consumed
In the fire of your nuclear presence,
You, my sun goddess,
My burning light of passion,
You, my love.

I'll speak to you in whispers of the heart,

Let you know how beautiful you are,

That you are precious,

Diamond eyes shining

With the light of your many facets,

Illuminating all that you are;

An angel in a world of grey,

Bringing colour and vitality to all you meet,

Your smile a beacon

In the gloom.

Sunlight skips along the collapsing crest of a wave,

Dances in my eyes

In the gentle hours of late afternoon,

As I sit amidst the rocks,

Her presence within me,

My gaze lost to the world

as it turns inwards,

To see your face,

Always.

I long to feel your breasts against my chest,
Our bodies joined in delectable union,
Moving with the rhythm of our love,
All that we are in wondrous harmony,
As we melt into each other,
In the heat of our passion,
The world lost to us,
Our essences shared in the flush of pleasure,
When our eyes become naked,
Our flames become entwined,
The act of love the completion of our beautiful union.

The sky is bejewelled in the diamond hours of darkness,

As we lie atop the hill side by side,

Feeling the warmth of each other's closeness,

Sharing a whispering silence,

As we sigh softly into the universe before us,

Aged starlight tumbling into our eyes,

Finding itself home after journeying a million miles and more.

We turn to each other,

Find the universe captured in our eyes,

The light of love sparkling,

Home at last.

Spun within the silk of moonlight,
We lie cocooned in each other's gaze
Atop the coastal hill awash with the sound of waves,
Adrift upon the ocean of our love.

You look deep within me and whisper 'yes'
In acceptance of all that I am,
A tear glitters in my eye
Before marking a solitary path upon my cheek.

You lean forward beneath the blanket of the night,
Take up the liquid fragility with your lips
As you kiss me with tenderness,
Taking ownership of all my joy, all my pain,
All my yesterdays and all my dreams for tomorrow,
Every element of my being
Gathering in the aspect of your eyes,
Beneath the unblinking moon,
Its illumination as nothing
Compared to the light within our hearts.

We melt into each other's presence,

The embrace a delicious sigh of union,

The fulfilment of longing,

As our warmth becomes one,

Our flames entwined,

Writhing together in breathless caresses,

Fingertips filled with the electricity of seduction,

Lips filled with the fire of love,

Flesh to flesh in a rapture of touches,

Lost in the naked immediacy,

In the sensations of pleasure so sweet,

Dripping from our bodies in liberation,

The honey of our desire,

As we move to the rhythm of creation,

Our bodies, hearts and minds interlocked,

This the intimacy of love,

Expressed in the poetry of our movements,

Climbing to the height of release,

When we collapse into the infinity of each other's eyes.

Beneath the Moon

The moon shimmers on the calm waters
Of the gently sighing Atlantic,
It caresses the sand with cool lips
And our lips press close in a warm embrace.

We lay upon the shore
Under the watchful gaze of the maiden of the sky,
The breeze touched with the growing warmth of spring
As it strokes our bare skin.

In timeless moments of union
We become joined in body and soul,
The rhythm of the ocean
Reflected in the calm rhythm of our pleasure,
As we make love upon the sands,
Robed in pale moonlight,
Our eyes shining with the light of love.

The door opens to reveal your smile,

Our pulses racing in night's hushed expectancy,

Our yearning finding its fulfilment,

As we stand before each other

In the truth of Now,

Oceans unable to keep us apart,

Unable to quench the flames

Burning within our hearts,

Entwining as we softly fall

Into the warm depths of our first embrace,

Tears of homecoming

Glistening with unspoken joy, as we are rekindled

Within the womb of each other's eyes,

Where the light of adoration burns

With consuming intensity,

Our phoenix wings opening

As we rise from the ashes of the past,

Take to the skies as one,

Our rebirth complete

In the glory of our love.

The oceanic waters of my heart,
Are filled with the refracted light
Of a treasure that shall always remain;
A love that shall endure.

The tide of time moves on,
But this love is constant,
Its continued presence within my depths a certainty,
Its existence evident in the sparkle of my eyes.

This love, this precious treasure
Within the pure waters of my heart,
Is for you and forever.

A white ship graces the horizon,
Drawing closer as its sails catch the warm breeze,
The ocean sedate in glittering beauty,
Capturing the dancing sunlight which fills our eyes,
We, two lovers perched on rocks,
Watching as the bow of the ship
Parts the waters in calm motion,
A sense of peace filling us,
As the sound of the fluttering sails
Becomes audible above the gentle tide
Which sighs upon the beach before us.

We turn as one and drift
On the oceans within our eyes,
The shimmering waters of our contentment,
The sails of our cleansed hearts
Filled with the breath of our love,
Thankful that the tidal currents of our lives
Have united us for now and evermore.

Exhalation

In the mist of a still morning,
As the hushed sound of gentle waves
Breaks upon my still form,
I see your face,
I see your beauty in the paleness,
An apparition drifting in my eyes,
Rising from the depths of my heart.

I stand naked in the soft caress of the mist,
The tide washing my bare feet
With its chill rise and fall.

I open my arms and walk forward,
Feeling the water gently accepting me
Into the growing depth,
The world about me veiled
As I see you swimming in the shallow swell,
So near, but out of reach,
The water at my throat and calling me on.

(*Exhalation continued*)

I vanish beneath the waves,

Find you waiting there,

Your arms outstretched,

Holding the promise of loves' embrace

In the timelessness of my last breath.

Love Eternal

Mist caresses the surface of the lake,
A blanket paled by the fading light of dusk,
As we sit side by side,
Arms about each other in the hush,
A bird flutters in nearby trees
As it settles for the night,
Crickets chirrup in the grasses
Upon the shoreline,
Where the water laps calmly
And captures the light of the rising moon.

We turn to each other,
The years fading away
As we fall into the light within each other's eyes,
The light of a love that has awoken
After a long slumber,
The light of a love that has forever been
And forever will be,
Its beauty and wonder shining in the corridors of time.

Beautiful Simplicity

We are softly caressed by starlight
As we walk along the shore,
The night succulent with the sound of sighing waves,
Our hands held, reflecting the bond
Of our hearts and minds,
A silence of contentment draped upon our shoulders,
Like a cloak that trails behind us
With the fading warmth of our bodies.

The call of a gull drifts over the ocean
And we pause to look seaward,
The horizon paled by the rising moon,
Which is lit by the light within our hearts,
More radiant than the sun,
Seen in our eyes as we face each other,
Break our silence in order to simply say
'I love you.'

Book Three

NIGHT WHISPERS

I go to the embrace of my dreams
And hope to feel your arms around me
In the stillness of the night,
When all that stirs is my heart,
Speaking your name into the silence,
Hearing your hushed reply
As it glides across the ocean,
To settle upon my sleeping form
With a sigh of contentment.

I go to the embrace of my dreams
To be with you, my love.

In the silence of the moment

You come to me,

Drift into my mind,

A being of luminescence,

Radiant in your robes of love,

A flowing gown of pure white

Which caresses my thoughts,

Eases the yearning

With the whisper of its movements,

Drawing my consciousness to my heart,

Urging me to follow you there,

So that I may find you dwelling

In the warmth of my being,

So I may be reminded that we are never truly parted,

That we are and shall forever remain

One.

He found her heart weeping in the dappled shade beneath the mournful branches of a willow on the banks of a stream.

He picked it up with fingers as gentle as the down of a newborn swan and raised it to his lips as its weeping abated.

The caress was like a sigh passing into a still night as he kissed her heart, the warmth of his touch filled with a love which would last forever.

With that first caress of his lips she knew she would weep no more.

Back in her chest he laid her heart, starting her soul anew.

His kiss had breathed life back into a body given up for dead. Raised from the grave an angel, a spirit, a woman. His for all time.

Your smile is a lullaby by which I have endless dreams of you,
Your picture an addiction from which I cannot tear my gaze,
Your eyes call me and I never wish to to turn away,
You the siren of my love, the cauldron of my desire,
You the alpha and omega of my existence,
You, the love of my life.

Your voice is the sound my heart makes when I smile,
Your words cause my breathing to slow.
Your smile quickens my pulse.
You are my joy.
Exultation!

Her voice, her voice,

I hear it echoing in my soul,

My heart answering the call,

My heart thunderous and swollen with her presence,

My heart, my heart,

Filled with love that knows no bounds,

And a fire that burns fiercely,

Crackling and consuming as I wait

For her arrival.

I have been slumbering, but now I awake

To her; the woman of my dreams now dwelling in my heart and soul.

Longing for You

The wind and ocean roar
In the darkness of night's stormy cloak,
A chill in the air
Forcing people to huddle into their clothes,
Seeking the meagre warmth of their bodies
Within the scant protection,
As they hurry to their destinations
And I watch from the hilltop;
A wild man hidden in the shadows
Of heavy clouds that begin to weep.

The rain becomes a downpour that beats
And bursts upon my pale face,
Whipped upon my skin by the howling gale,
My arms opening wide and coat snapping
In desperate twists and turns at my back,
My eyes turning to gaze west
Across white peaked waves,
My mouth opening wide and lungs emptying
As I call your name.

From Out of the Mist

Mist hugs the shoreline,
A white blanket with moist lips,
Caressing me as I stand on the beach,
A vague apparition amidst the paleness,
Lacking solidity, softened
As the sounds of the breaking surf
Wash gently through the veil
That hides the world from my gaze.
Through the mist I see a figure,
A ghost drifting along the sands,
Moving towards me in the pale hush,
My pulse rising as your face becomes clear,
Smiling, eyes like beacons
That call me safely home
Into your waiting arms,
Holding the promise of love's deliverance,
The mist clearing as the breath of our desire
Turns the dream into reality.

The Thief I Desire

With a sequential turn of keys
The safe breaker has an easy task,
As she plies her trade with dexterity,
For I handed her the keys,
And now she is ready to step inside.

She is in,
She is in,
A thief has entered my heart,
Is stealing all that I have,
And I am glad.

Wooden Cup

I am but a wooden cup,
Roughly carved and without varnish.

It is my emptiness that makes me useful,
That can be filled with inspiration;
The touch of the divine
That seeks to touch others.

I am but a wooden cup,
Filled with the inspiration of you,
And the sparkling water of love.

I wake beside her and smile,

For there is such joy in her presence,

In the sight of her softly breathing,

Eyes still closed to the waking world,

She slumbers in dreams

That leave the faintest trace of a smile upon her lips,

Our bed one of contentment,

Our contentment a bed of love.

♥♥♥

She comes to me in the darkness,

Cloaked in stars,

Robed in glittering beauty,

Her light illuminating my face,

Bringing the gift of her love

As my heart pounds her name.

She is my light in the darkness,

My love of every breath.

Awakening in a Golden Dawn

The poet within awakens,
In the dawn of love's true light,
Wishing to express feelings
That are truly beyond words,
Trying to grasp emotions
That are beyond reach.

The poet within awakens,
Breathes upon the page,
Speaks the language of love,
Yearning to touch your heart,
To caress your soul,
Every word a pale reflection
Of my feelings for you, my everything.

Dreams

Come away with me

In my dreams,

And we will ride the ocean

Atop dolphins glittering in the moonlight,

We will fly amongst the stars on comets,

Writing 'I love you' with their bright tails,

We will laugh as we slide

Down the colours of a rainbow,

We will lie peacefully beside each other

Upon a bed of flowers

Caressing us with morning dew.

Come away with me

And I will make your life a dream come true.

Upon the Ocean

If I could put a message in a bottle
And knew it would reach your shore,
I'd place my heart upon the ocean,
To be ushered to you by the breath of my desire,
Guided by the current of my love,
To arrive upon your golden sands,
And be taken into your trembling hands,
As you listen to it's pulse
And hear it beating your name.

Limitless Bed of Dreams

I mumble in my sleep,
She pushes me in hers,
Half-awake, half-asleep,
We travel in different directions
As if the bed were limitless,
An endless expanse in the night
Where dreams stretch out to the sides,
Lay upon the covers beside us
As we curl and uncurl,
Turn and return,
Mumble and snort,
Snore and nudge,
Spend the night in a limitless bed,
In the morning to find
The bed limited once more,
And yet...
And yet each day is a dream come true
As long as I wake beside her.

Morning Hush

I sigh in the morning hush
As day breaks so softly,
Its light growing with the gentle persuasion
Of the rising sun,
My heart fluttering on wings of velvet
That beat your name,
Images of you drifting into my mind
As the diffused light of day grows ever brighter,
To reveal you beside me,
Your breath a shallow rise and fall
As you dream in restfulness,
A contented smile upon your beautiful countenance.

I sigh in the morning hush.
Filled with the joy of waking to a new day
By your side.

From Dreams to Reality

Run away with me into our dreams,

Take my hand and open your wings,

Stretch them wide to catch on the wind

Of our love as it blows warm and free

Across the ocean that divides us,

Across the expanse that can never keep us apart,

For tonight we may only meet in our dreams,

But tomorrow we shall meet in the truth of Now.

In Winter's Chill

In winter's bony chill
I stare at the trees beyond the window,
That stretch barren limbs
Towards the cloud-veiled sun,
My gaze fixed upon the distant horizon,
Where sky and ocean draw together
In a grey embrace,
The hidden sun sinking towards its watery demise
In cold arms of pastel hues.

As the velvet dark
Spreads its blanket over the world,
I find warmth growing within my heart,
Its existence evident in my every breath,
Each exhalation caressing your name
In whispered softness,
My pulse like the ocean tides
Now hidden from my sight by night's arrival.

(In Winter's Chill continued)

The trees turn their branches towards me in the darkness,
Sense the warmth and light within my breast,
Radiating from a love so glorious
That the sun is but a flake of winter snow in comparison.

My heart calls out in the darkness,

But there is no answer, only silence,

As I strain to hear a sound,

Still feeling you within me,

Still exhaling you with every breath,

Though feeling the touch of loneliness,

A chill caress in the night,

While I yearn for your words,

Ache for your actions,

Through these long hours

That shuffle languidly towards the inevitable dawn,

When I will wake alone.

I hear you breathing next to me in the darkness,
Turning, I find the bed empty,
Feel a pang on loneliness,
But know that emptiness
Holds the promise
Of your presence,
As does the emptiness within my arms
That will be filled by you,
Echoing the fullness of my heart;
This place within me where you dwell.

I wait for the day
When you are in my bed and in my arms,
I wait for the day
And know I will never be able to let you go.

A Dream

If this be a dream
Then let me never wake,
Let me remain in the embrace
Of your arms and your eyes,
Let me rest my head against your chest
And hear you heart beating my name
In the darkest hours,
Let me wake beside you with the morning light
And stroke your pale cheek
With the affection of a lover's touch.

If this be a dream
Then let me never wake,
For a dream of you
Is better than a lifetime alone.

Sarah woke softly. Dreams tumbled silently from her sleep-messed blonde hair. Turning, she reached out and found the other side of the bed empty and its coldness betrayed the span of time's passage.

Slowly opening her eyes, she glanced at the space beside her and then looked to the window beyond, pale curtains slightly parted to reveal a day of labouring clouds beyond, their bellies dark as they pressed in on the world beneath. She sighed, a slight frown upon her face in the gloom, the room about her lacking definition in the dullness of the new day.

Her stomach groaned and, setting her jaw against the cold she knew was to come, she rose and climbed out from beneath the deep blue covers. The chill wrapped itself about her bare arms and calves, running its invisible fingers across her skin and making her tremble.

Quickly stepping to the door, she took down her pale pink dressing gown and wrapped it about herself, snuggling into its embrace with a passing look of contentment.

The soft frown of sadness returned. She opened the door and walked out upon the landing. The house was filled with silence.

Passing along the landing, she entered the bathroom and pulled the light cord, electric brightness quickly chasing away the dullness of the day, forcing its retreat to beyond the small window opposite her. She glanced at the window, her eyes reflecting the sadness of her frown, and then stepped to the sink.

Sarah looked into the mirror before her and her eyes widened in shock. Her pulse quickened and she blinked a few times, believing she was still dreaming.

The sight in the mirror persisted. It was an image of herself in a different bathroom. Sunshine was slanting in through the window in a beam of rich gold. The decor was different, as was her appearance. Her other self was naked and comfortable in her nudity, her movements betraying no self-consciousness. There was a lightness to her other self, an ease of movement accompanied by a smile and a sparkle in her eyes, the intensity of which she'd never witnessed before.

Sarah closed her eyes and shook her head, trying to shake the image from her mind. Slowly opening her eyes once more, she tentatively looked into the mirror to find her other self standing right before her, looking straight at her.

'Hello?' she said with soft trepidation.

Her other self did not respond, looked straight through Sarah while running fingers through her hair, clearly watching herself in what must have been the mirror in her own bathroom.

'I can see her, but she can't see me,' thought Sarah, feeling a pang of longing as she saw such happiness in the expression of her other self.

Slowly, as if not wishing to scare off the wonderful vision of such brightness, Sarah raised her right hand and began to reach towards the image. Her fingers trembling slightly as they neared the mirror, she found herself holding her breath. The tips of her fingers tingled and then came into contact with the coldness.

A sudden jolt ran through her and Sarah stepped back from the mirror in surprise. She blinked a few times and stared at her face, a look of slight confusion shown in her reflection.

The door opened and she turned to find Pete entering, stepping into a beam of sunlight that lay its golden touch upon his bare skin.

'Are you okay?' he asked with concern, noticing the slightly perplexed expression upon her face.

The strange feeling that had come over her was rapidly dissipating into the warmth of the room, the chill that had run the length of her spine already a memory. 'It's nothing,' she said as her bright smile returned, the recollection of a former existence melting away like a ghost shrinking from the dawning sun.

Pete walked over to stand behind her, slipping his arms about her waist, their naked bodies pressed close. He looked at her reflected face over her shoulder and they smiled at each other, their eyes locked and filled with love's desire. He kissed her bare neck and then locked his gaze with hers once more.

'I love you,' he whispered into her ear, his breath upon her skin and the soft sound of the words making her shiver as her heart overflowed and its light flooded the room.

Homeward Bound

I hear the wind,

Your voice whispering in its passing,

Calling me across the ocean to your arms,

To the embrace of the love

That burns like a beacon on your distant shore,

Guiding me through the night,

My ship upon the waters of our unity,

Its sails filled with the wind of your beauty,

As I journey to your side,

Knowing I am coming home at last.

Lucid Dream

In the softness of a lucid dream
We are together,
We find the unity promised
In half-heard whispers
That I follow like a wraith
Along the corridors of time,
Longing to hold your truth in my arms,
To feel your breath upon my skin,
To see the light in your eyes
As it surrounds me
And I am engulfed in the wonder of our love.

In the softness of a lucid dream
I find you,
Until the day when I take you in my arms
And we share the truth of all we are
In the eternal moment of our union.

My precious ghost, my beautiful wraith,

You surround me in your light

Till the early hour when you depart,

Fading from my room,

But always shining in my heart,

Where I'll keep you

Until I can hold you in my arms

And never let you go.

If you are but a dream then I do not wish to wake,

As I slumber in the depths of your eyes,

A soft lullaby sung by your smile,

My singularity becoming lost in your embrace,

Overcome by a sense of belonging,

For at last I have found my way home...

...to you.

If you are but a dream,

I will sleep

Forever in your arms.

He stands before the bathroom mirror
And smiles, hair ruffled
By dreams of her, sure he can spy
The passage of her playful fingers,
Sure he can feel the touch of her lips
Upon his skin, lingering
Now the dreams have faded,
As she lingers, sweet love
Dwelling in his heart and soul,
Visible in his eyes as he stares
Into the depths of his reflection,
Content in the knowledge that the dreams may fade,
But love, sweet love, will always remain.

The photograph speaks to me
In whispers of love's longing.
I gaze into your eyes,
Wish I could remain lost within their depths
Forever,
Wish I could reach out and stroke your cheek,
As I catch the scent of your perfume
On the gentle breeze of our movements,
My fingers trembling against the warmth of your cheeks,
The sound of your breathing soft upon my heart,
Which swells with your presence,
With the closeness of our existence,
In this vision, this dream
Of a photograph becoming real.

Calling Your Name

White crests ride the waves,
Horses galloping upon the ocean,
Moonlit in the darkness as I stand upon the cliffs,
My gaze cast westward,
Knowing you are there, beyond the horizon,
Knowing that each second brings us closer
To the first embrace,
When we become entwined in totality,
Our union complete.

The waves crash upon the shore
Beneath the bluffs where I stand,
I call your name and the sound is taken
In the arms of the westerly wind,
Knowing your heart will hear it
And answer in kind.

If I could swim the ocean to be by your side,
I'd dive from the cliff-tops to be embraced by the cold waters,
Knowing that your warm embrace would be waiting
Upon the distant shore.

If I had wings with which to take to the sky,
I'd spread them wide and glide from the bluffs,
My shadow racing across the waves
To be by your side.

I stare out to sea and imagine diving from the cliffs,
Envisage plunging into the waters or opening my wings,
Longing to be with you and to take you in my arms,
To find myself at home within your embrace,
And, in truth, I know that even the widest ocean
Could never keep our love apart,
That the day of our union will come
And the waters will evaporate in the first touch of our lips.

I strayed into the orchard of your dream to find you dancing amidst the whispering trees, bare feet lifting upon the warm breeze as a song hung in the air and beams of sunlight sparkled in the depths of your eyes, pale blossom softly caressing your face as your white gown flowed behind you and marked the wake of your joyous passage, butterflies weaving their flutters about the tendrils of your streaming hair.

I strayed into the orchard and now we dance together, sharing this dream called life and savouring the fruit of every moment, every breath part of the song of existence.

My breath is the flutter of your heart

As my lips tenderly follow your curves,

Cooling saliva left in their pouting wake,

My eyes closed as I draw in the scent of you,

Filled with your immediacy;

The warmth of your skin,

The sigh of your desire,

The movement of your longing,

The moments of timelessness

In a world all our own,

Our bodies entwined

In the night we come to possess.

She lies naked before him in the candlelight,
Earth mother, fire woman,
Waiting for his touch so desired,
As he devours her with his hungry gaze.

She quivers as his fingers delight upon her skin,
Water lady, air maiden,
As he bows his head in worship,
Kisses her breasts in cooling sensitivity.

Earth, fire, water, air,
She the elemental awakened by his touch,
As he makes love to her in the embracing darkness,
His penetration the final connection,
Every aspect of who they are now entwined
Forevermore.

A delightful joy is entwined by soft sadness
In the succulence of the night,
As she comes to me through the darkness
And my spirit soars on wings thought clipped,
Spreading them wide in angelic countenance:
Her words their wind on which to rise,
Her eyes the infinity to be explored,
Her smile the warmth of distant hope.

Then she softly departs and my wings enfold,
Soft sadness caressing my heart,
Where her name is whispered with such delight,
Though touched with a melancholy which shall pass,
When the light of day finally touches our faces
And we stand together beneath the sun,
No longer trapped by the darkness and the distance,
But released into each other's arms.

My velvet heart holds you in its soft embrace,

Its warm pulse my every breath,

As I breathe the oxygen of our love in night's hushed reverence,

Where no wind stirs bar my gentle exhalation of your name,

Before I inhale the starlight with my gaze,

The beauty of the heavens hung upon your image

In the depths of my eyes,

As the moon rises in misted pale,

Reflecting the sun's light like a mirror laced with dust,

Just as I reflect your light, my love,

For you are the sun and I the moon

Orbiting the wonder of your existence.

What if I were to walk through the veil of your dreams and kiss the tears of yesterday from your cheeks? What if I were to light the candle of my heart so you may be guided to its warming flame? What if I were to walk through the mists of unfolding time and take your hand so we may walk together? What if I were to open my wings and turn to you with infinity within my eyes? Would you smile in your bed of dreams? Would you bring your flame to mine and let them entwine? Would you walk with me through the mists of tomorrow's mystery? Would you take my hand and open your wings so we may fly into the sparkling infinity of each other's eyes?

I found her heart alone in the wilderness,
Crying in the darkness,
Not daring to hope as it shivered in the cold.

My heart ached in recognition
Of its own condition,
Saw the truth of a wondrous light within.

In the beating of our hearts
We had communion,
Shared our light in the darkness and felt it grow.

Its brightness surrounded us,
Chasing away the night in its glory,
Bringing warmth and growth where there had been none.

We shared our hearts in the moment,
Our union becoming stronger as dawn promised a new day,
Our heartbeats becoming the shared pulse of love.

One Heart

I am a captive of your eyes,

A prisoner of your beauty,

Held in the bonds of all that shines from you,

Caught in the light that surrounds me

In the warmth of who you are,

Seen so clearly from afar,

This my waking dream from which I wish no escape,

Your face caressed by my thoughts,

My flame entwined with yours,

As two hearts pulse with the wonder of love,

As two hearts

Become one.

Neo-Cortex Synapses

I am without eyes, yet see her face.
I am without ears, yet hear her voice.
I am without arms, yet hold her close.
I am without lips, yet kiss her tenderly.

Synapses fire in hidden silence,
My eyelids fluttering during REM sleep,
Electricity pulsing in rapid translation,
My desire for her
So deep it lies beyond consciousness.

During sleep my mind undergoes devolution from my body,
No sensory system is necessary by which to see her,
Hear her, hold her, kiss her,
For she abides in my neo-cortex,
Until my eyelids snap open
And I find her lying beside me.

I want to raise the sun into your skies,

Bring joy to the sparkle of your eyes,

Brighten your every waking day,

Chase all the dark clouds far away.

I want to give you love with no condition,

Banish doubt and superstition,

Fill your heart with radiant light,

That will shine through every day and every night.

I want to give you all I have to give,

Show you what it means to truly live,

In the wonder of a love so true,

A love whose name is you.

Ablaze

Wrapped in silence,
Soundless, wordless darkness,
Drifting, floating without resistance
Into the unknown, the unseen,
A faint light sparks into existence
In the far distance,
I blink and wonder if it is real,
As the currents of my life
Take me ever closer
Through the void, through the pitch
Which is pierced by the growing brightness,
Sparkling like a star of burning fire,
Holding the promise of a warm embrace,
Its beauty blinding, heat reaching out to me
With invisible fingers
That usher away the cold,
My eyes wide as the star grows
To fill my blazing vision, I see
One flame coiled and turning,

(Ablaze continued)

One flame entwined about itself
Creating a ball of fire, a wonderful intensity.

An arch of flame bursts forth in the darkness,
Engulfing me, enveloping me
In light and heat,
Igniting all that I am,
So that I begin to burn, my flame renewed,
The dark no longer holding sway
As my flame entwines with yours,
Two stars now bright in the depths
Of time's great span.

She walked through the Cornish seaside town, a vision of beauty robed in mist. Her feet were bare and she wore a simple dress of blue which looked translucent in the white breath of the world. Her black hair glistened with drops of moisture; liquid diamonds capturing the world in their gentle sparkle.

The sound of waves gently breathing on the shore drifed through the paled surroundings as she walked on, her step assured, heart leading her without need for conscious direction.

Soon she descended onto the sands of the beach, the sound of the sea growing more distinct. The surf became visible through the veil and a shadow shood in the caress of the waters, opaque and still.

She smiled, no pause in her step, only a measured movement towards the man who stood before her. Drawing up beside him, she took his hand in hers and he turned.

'It's beautiful,' he said with reverencial breathlessness.

She smiled and leant forward. They kissed softly and the blanket of mist wrapped itself about them.

'How did you find me in this?' he asked.

'I just followed my heart,' she replied. 'I'm surprised I didn't make you jump.'

'I was listening to mine,' he said, 'and it told me you were coming.'

She smiled, eyes and hair glittering.

They turned to the sea and began to walk deeper into the waters. It's surface tension rose up their bodies until the moment when they slipped into the waves and vanished beneath the surface.

Gracefully risng into the air, two dolphins glistened as they danced and played in the waves, vanishing into the mists which cast their magic over the world, existing out of time as they swam in the ocean of possibility.

Beneath the Moon

In the dearest sunset
I have ever known,
We held each other tight,
Watched day pass
In vivid hues upon high clouds,
Then night enfolded us in dark robes
And we kissed beneath the rising moon,
That leant its mercury glow
To our warm embrace.

Your morning smile
Is the sunrise,
It is the birdsong greeting each new day,
It is the joy of waking beside you
For the rest of my life.

Your morning smile
Is my reason to wake,
Finding myself bathed in your light,
Hearing your song of beauty,
Feeling the joy of the love we share.

The Flutter of Golden Lashes

In the mornings,
When golden light falls
Upon your sleepy face,
I leave a touch of mercury
Upon your lips,
As I kiss them tentatively,
As if afraid
To find you a figment of my imagination.

You stir and briefly smile,
I turn and tip-toe from our room,
Already dreaming of my return.

You are my dream and my reality,

You are my alpha and omega,

I could not wish for more,

Would not,

For in you I have found

My everything.

The Mists of tomorrow part slowly
Upon the plain of my life,
A figure emerging from their concealment,
Vague at first, ghostly
In its hushed approach,
Drifting towards me in robes of certainty and silence,
The mist clinging like pale hands
Unable to stop the march of time,
As the figure draws closer,
From what is to be
Into what simply is,
The grip of the mist receding
To reveal your face, my love,
As you walk into my waiting arms.

The sea breeze stirs the sands of my heart,
As it whispers your name in the twilight of day's passing,
And I yearn for you to visit my shores.

The night wraps me in dark arms of longing,
As I lay my head to rest
And stare at the space before me where you will one day lie.

I close my eyes to find you waiting in my dreams,
Sailing upon the ocean of my subconscious,
Your sails bright as you approach my shore.

I hear your voice in the darkness,
You call to me from the light of my dreams;
'Love, I am here, I am with you.'

If you enjoyed this book then try the novels *Heart's Desire* and *Fey* or the novella *For Love or Money*. They are among the many books by Edwin Page that are available on Kindle and as paperbacks.

18589467R00092

Printed in Great Britain
by Amazon